I Can't Wait to See My Wings...

The Chrysalis Chronicles
A Collection of Poems

J A Smith

authorHOUSE®

AuthorHouse™
1663 Liberty Drive
Bloomington, IN 47403
www.authorhouse.com
Phone: 1 (800) 839-8640

Published by AuthorHouse   05/08/2017

ISBN: 978-1-5246-8994-0 (sc)
ISBN: 978-1-5246-8992-6 (hc)
ISBN: 978-1-5246-8993-3 (e)

Library of Congress Control Number: 2017906604

Print information available on the last page.

Any people depicted in stock imagery provided by Thinkstock are models, and such images are being used for illustrative purposes only. Certain stock imagery © Thinkstock.

This book is printed on acid-free paper.

CONTENTS

For "Lissa"

INTRODUCTION

People have always been delighted by the beauty of a butterfly. Butterflies are considered to be one of the most beautiful insects in the world. In many cultures they symbolize rebirth, and the transformation from youth into adult-hood and maturation.

What begins as a starving caterpillar, one day, stops eating and hangs upside down from a tree, wraps itself into a cocoon, or chrysalis, and initiates the concealed transformation into an eye-catching butterfly. You wouldn't know it by looking at them, but some caterpillars have primitive tiny wings tucked inside their bodies. When metamorphosis is complete the butterfly emerges from the chrysalis, and uses its muscles to pump blood through its body and wings to prepare to fly. The radical process a caterpillar endures to become a butterfly is hidden and unbelievable but the results are magnificent.

Just as a caterpillar does, we, as people all have our periods of intense growth. I think the most critical stages of growth are spent in isolation and silence, quite like a caterpillar in a chrysalis. However, as people we spend that time looking inward as well as outward. We begin to reflect on the lessons we learned, the trials we've faced, and the monumental milestones in life we've conquered. We begin to look at our current relationships with our family, significant others, *babies-mama or babies-daddies*, our friends, the people around us, and even our past relationships. We reflect on where we went wrong, and rejoice in the times when things went right. Or even when things began wrong, but turned out right. We begin to observe our surroundings, the things that take place

in our environments, on our televisions, and the media outputs. It's so easy to become entrenched these days by technology and the things that we see. One must develop a deeper sense of security, understanding, and revelation in regards to the things that we can be "force-fed" as a nation. Sometimes we struggle with a difference in opinion, or perspective on things. So we search to understand things as we see them or better yet as we may perceive them. We also begin to struggle with spiritual war-fare and our religion. It becomes either a first-nature for some, second nature for others, or completely obsolete. This may be up for debate in other cases. I myself, know that I can do absolutely NOTHING without God. So when this transformation takes place and we've embarked on new periods of enlightenment, we see things from a higher perspective, a different angle. The view is rather amazing when you transcend from the ground to the sky!!!

PROLOGUE

No way to see beyond the realm of reality
But many visions created to call this an extravagant fantasy
Or a dream you may call it, something beautiful and perfect
A life far away, but the distance is definitely worth it
A strong urge to bring the distance into existence
But merely all, just seems fictional
Green grass, blue skies, all objects three dimensional
Looking beyond the silver lining
To a complete and perfect world
Dreams of the adult with no imagination
But still I'm merely just a little girl
What doesn't kill the caterpillar will transform it into a
butterfly
It's amazing the transformation it takes to go from the
ground to the sky!!!

CHAPTER 1

Philophobia

No Place for a Heart of Gold

This world isn't a place for a heart of gold
Feelings are so warm, but the world and it's "creatures" are
so cold
I'm struggling to fit the mold
Can't put away the instinct God gave me
But haven't found one that equals the definition for "Loyalty"
Sitting here with tears in my eyes cause I'm so bruised
Can't talk to anyone cause no one ever knows what to do
When your emotions run deep, people can't relate to you
You're just living everyday yearning to have back what
you're putting out
But REAL isn't what anyone is about
Talk is cheap, but actions are expensive
I'm trying to send a message here, pay attention
How does one love but pause to trust
Do you really understand the difference between love and lust?
The "creatures" creating false relationships, selling dreams,
and buying them back
what part of the game is that?
What happens to the ones with the hearts of gold?
Searching for someone with whom they can grow old
not interested in the "*game*" or any of the "*players*"
Just simply peeling off the many, many layers
How do you survive when love is your oxygen?
But you're living in a time where the air is thin.....

Selfish

When you do the things you do
Appears as if the only person you consider first is you
Never once attempting to take thought in the fact
That there is simply something wrong with that
Minor things you miss and most big situations as well
Simply put, you are selfish as hell
Never wanting to sacrifice a fraction of your time, for
someone you claim you love
But heaven forbid they do the same, or even have a mere
thought of
Narcissistic in so many individual ways
Such as missing important events or forgetting special days
Doing little infinite things that you would hate the next for
Exhibiting characteristics of hypocrisy and then much more
And oh, let no one dare bring your transgressions to the
forefront of your attention
Since you are the way you are, there are no guidelines or
means of redemption
That's what makes it much worst, you are ok with what you do
You see nothing that you do as wrong, as long as it's all
about you
It never crosses your mind to think how your actions may
have affected others
At least until they treat you the same, then we have a major
game of blame
Please don't make rules of relationships that you only intend
to break
And don't continue to expect others to keep giving, if all
you do is take!!!

Emotionless

You couldn't blame her for being numb to this shit
No, she's not trying to be a bitch, but if so she has 100
reasons ready to list
Bounced back a few times, thinking this time it's going to
change
And each time she witnessed a greater sense of pain
She developed a hate for the art of the heart
She said "It ain't never done nothing but rip me apart"
Now she knew she wasn't perfect, but real, and that's a fact
Man writing this is crazy
Because I'm still wounded from the impact
All the time, blood, sweat, and tears
And the one thing she thought was a constant, became her
biggest fear
Crippled for life and constantly guarded
She prayed every day because she knew God didn't want
her to be cold-hearted
But lord knows it's hard
She could never inflict the pain that was inflicted on her
And hell that's the hard part
If you only knew what she felt
Playing all the cards she had been dealt
She said "see when you give "*them*" all of you, you ain't got
a damn thing left over"
I guess that's the consequences of wearing the ol' ticker on
your shoulder
Now I'm walking around with blood all over ME
As the unmarked evidence of love's greatest tragedy.

Philophobia

I'm not afraid of pain, it's love that terrifies me
The feelings behind it all provokes suspense, a thriller, an all-out mystery
Is it merely just a dream?
Or is it a colorful, visual thing?
A rainbow spectrum of colors, however they say a percentage of colors we see aren't really there
We make them up mentally and visually, dismissing the fact that all things are actually white and bare
I'm not afraid of pain, I'm afraid to care
What is this they speak of?
Who is they? You interrupt to ask
The outsiders, the others, the people behind the glass
Staring at me like I'm a catastrophe
Something straight out of the hell of another galaxy
Ok, well back to the question at hand
Love, they call it, this thing known to man
It seems so temporary, so conditional, so over abused, and misused
But you long for it and crave it, and without it you sing the color of the blues
I think it's all just a hoax, a way to keep you enslaved
A way to plot deaths, with blood filled graves
I'm not afraid of pain, it's love that terrifies me
I'm the offspring of pain, from when love was conceived
You won't get this, it's of another realm
Sometimes my thoughts tend to get dim, and grow grim
I start speaking from an alter ego, my Dr. Jekyll goes crazy
And Mr. Hyde goes wild

I stand in the infinite space between the coherent adult and an innocent unknowledgeable child
I'm not afraid of pain, it's love that keeps me terrified
I never fear the betrayal of pain, for she always sticks around
It's love that always seems lost, and nowhere to be found.....

It's worth the fight

Every day won't be a good day
And every day won't be the same
But stop acting like I don't see that things have changed
Emotionally detached, zoned-out, non-communicative and
distant
This is far from the definition of consistent
You say I push you away, and I say you don't notice me
I'm sure we're both beginning to wonder if this is truly meant
to be
Laughter cut short, talks are few and far between
"I love you" are you sure that's what you really mean?
I'm tired, you're tired, and the storm has yet to begin
But late at night I'm knowing I need you, my lover, and my
friend
Something has to give, the ice has to break
This movie isn't over, this is only the first take
Get your head out your ass, and embrace what you have
I'm not her, you're not him, and this is present tense, not the
past
I understand I'm not easy, and you sir are no cake walk
All I'm asking you to do is communicate, you know how to
TALK
I need you to help me make things back right
Because you and I are certainly worth the fight.

We all we got

It's strange how things can change
The same things that make you laugh one day make you cry
And the same hellos are abruptly exchanged for good bye
Seasons come and go and yes's slowly turn into no's
And what was once considered "one" is now in two's
And in the middle is left, you!
You, all alone to soak up the pain
Walls soaked in hateful words like rain
Secrets told, hearts broken, and lives spinning out of control
I must admit, it really took a toll
I mean it really did, I don't think anybody really understood
the impact
Something easy to get over, for some, is an outsider's
opinion
NOT MY FACT!
I couldn't swallow enough happy meds
To silence the words I had been fed
Not enough couches and counselors in the world to heal
the trauma
Where do you hide when you're in the middle of your
parent's drama?
Whose side do you take when they both are wrong?
The days become dark and the nights grow long
You learn to cope
In the midst of it you keep hope
That one day the smoke will clear and things will mend
Until then you search for healing within
But then time goes by and we all begin to change, heal,
and grow
Red lights turn green, and stopped hearts all decide to go
Go back to a place, that's familiar but new and changed

See no matter what you do you can't forget your last name
You don't forget what made you family and what made you close
Things happen, and as for karma, we've all had a dose
You take the lesson, the stories, and you file them away
You bury them, in a faraway plot
And you NEVER forget that we all we got!

Gutter Love

Lost my heart to the streets, struggling to cope, but never losing hope
Aint been the same ever since, intense....
Heart luke warm, I say that with sarcastic charm
Simply because I'm in between heaven and hell
This isn't a dream I'm trying to sell
Somebody post my bail
Screaming "I NEED MY HEART BACK"
I'm thrown all off track
Got Gates playing in my ear, ayeeee, I'm in my feelings
This shit is too real, I'm on an emotional high, no ceilings
You don't know the pain!!!
This love was poison, toxic to my veins
But I couldn't pull back, the feelings had no reigns
I think I would've lost it all just to stay there
It was hell on earth, and the lord knew I didn't care
I need my heart back, this pain isn't fair....

Misandry

She didn't develop it on her own, or by some traumatic
incidents
It wasn't rape, sexual abuse, or any of those "only seen on
tv" type horrible events
Actually it derived from something that was so beautiful, at
least it appeared to be
But sometimes beauty is a makeup that hides misery
It seemed ok, but I guess the beginning always is
I remember her saying, you never really know a man until
you have his kids
A statement with a dry humor, if I do say so my self
She gave him her heart, with the intentions of NEVER giving
it to anyone else
She would sit in my office and ponder over and over, how it
all went bad
Some days I think it literally drove her mad
She loved him, and the thing that puzzled her most, is that
she knew that he loved her back
But he no longer knew how to treat her, and sadly she had
to face the fact
I tried to get her to understand that all of her feelings were ok
But I could see it was making her grow colder, with each
passing day
To be continued....

Weary Woman

Lord send me someone who will prove me wrong
Because lord knows I'm sick and tired of being strong
Tired of raising my kids alone
Tired of these men who only want to pretend
But turn so fake and fraud in the end
Tired of being the one who has it all together
Tired of these fake ass renditions of forever
I've always been a woman who was careful with my heart
I ain't got time to be playing the part
I'm not easily impressed, and at any ole thing, I'm not amused
But lord knows as for the few I've let in, I'm tired of being misused
Third times a charm, pretty sure I've said that once before
I'm not taking any more losses, not any more
I'm a quick learner, and bullshit is easy to peep
I'm not tolerating a liar, inconsistency, or a man that wants to creep
See unlike most in my generation, I'm not about to play any games
I don't need another motherfucker to obtain my fortune or fame
I can dance to my own beat, and I move fluently, as well
I'm not letting no man treat me like a fallen angel and drag me through hell
God made me from you, but you were born from my womb
Before I let one mistreat me, I'll see an early tomb
I don't want to play the victim, and being the villain is beneath my essence
I want someone who simply adores my existence and acknowledges my presence

One who recognizes my strength and capitalizes the fact that I'm zealous
Not a man who will half ass his efforts, then slick get jealous
I want someone who will listen to my heart and respect my mind
A man so hidden in God, I need the three disciples to find
One who understands that honesty and appreciation go a long way
One who shows gratitude and attentiveness even on a rough day
One who works as hard as I will, to take care of us
One who I can ultimately TRUST!!!

Get you a man

Get you a man that doesn't necessarily need you
That way, "you know it's real"
Get you a man that's not looking to sit at the table
And just partake in another hearty meal
One that's going to provide and help put food on the table
Not one who will act intellectually crippled and emotionally disabled
Get you a man that's going to pray for you
When the devil has you feeling really low
Not one that's going to have you on that "Barbra, this is Shirley" duet
Because he out acting like a hoe
Get you a man that doesn't require you questioning his integrity
One that's going to challenge you spiritually, emotionally, and also intellectually
One you can build with, without having to start from scratch
Stay away from the ones that can only show "love"
When you're lying on your back
Get you a man that's not into arguing and cussing
But one that knows how to communicate and handle a little fussing
Get you a man with a plan, a man that has some ambition
A man! Not a boy, a limited edition!!

Fine Vodka & Wine

Never give a vodka drinker fine wine
They won't be able to handle that shit when it's time
Time, time, time to show up and make things happen
This is becoming a problem, and you sitting there laughin'
You a drunk, drunk off your own lies and made up stories
And just like a drinker, you're showing all your glory
Vodka got you feeling yourself, but the taste you own is cheap
Just like the things you talk, your game has been peeped
You can't hold fine wine, at its finest it intoxicates you
You're inebriated to full capacity, stick to what you know boo
What's here will only make you sick
It's apparent by your staggering and stumbling
You're not ready for this...!!!

Victim of Love

She gave you six years of her life
Six years, and you abused her, that isn't right
Time after time, she's drying her eyes
Time after time, she's believing your lies
Praying for change and hoping for the best
Stressed over your foolish pride and losing her rest
Loving you from head to toe, flaws and all
Picking you up every time you fall
Building up your character, educating you with facts
But honesty and consistency, you continued to lack
Never once did she claim to be of perfect perfection
But she was never shy of loyalty, honesty, and protection
For you, she would do anything
Even withstand the pain and abuse you would bring
Never will she lie and just swear it was all bad
You could make her laugh from a healthy place
Even when you were the one who made her mad
She said "even his lies could sound so truthful"
I guess because it was you though
She mentioned, "I knew he had my back and would kill for me
But somewhere something changed and he became my
arch enemy"
You two had created a bond, or at least she guessed
Thirty nine weeks of hell and she gave you 7 pounds and 1
ounce of her best
Even through your absence and foolish ways through that
She believed deep down you could make a come back
She never cheated, but you accused her over and over
But your own guilt and insecurities,
For some, can create a chip on their shoulder
No matter the disrespect, nor the neglect
She still would include you in her prayers
Because she still seen you as the man she met...

31

CHAPTER 2

Memoirs to a "baby daddy"

A Single Mother's Struggle

Beautiful creations made out of love
But somewhere the love goes wrong between the two
So now the responsibility is on who?
A blessing gone wrong, that's constantly got you stressing
That's what you sometimes think, while your feelings are on ten
Because you have to make it happen for them day in and
day out and simply pretend
Pretend that the real hurt doesn't even exist
That the questions aren't unanswered, that the anger
doesn't burn inside
Struggling because you don't want to ask the Negro for
nothing
Some people having the nerve to call it pride
But the thought is, if he wanted to do, he would
Because they're your blessings too, so you should
The pain is, why you would turn your back, leaving your
children alone
Tossing and turning in your sleep every night
Mental, emotional, physical demons constantly looking for
a fight
The facades you see being put up, the lies you always hear
But never once stopping to drop a sweat or a tear
Constant conversations with God
Asking him for help and understanding
Trying to stay on top of a two person job alone can be quite
demanding
A prayer daily to bless the same person or persons who so
easily ripped your heart in half
This is a concept that the weak could never grab
Smiling when you really would rather die

Holding in the truth, because silence is more beautiful than a lie
All the while planning birthday parties alone
Paying the bills, over extending yourself to create a home
School activities, doctor appointments, and anything you can name
Doing it because this is your job, your purpose, your blessing
This isn't for social media fame
Doing everything in your power to be the best at this job you weren't prepared for
You have no instructions to use
A job between two, that began with "I love you"
And ended with it being all on you.

Memoir to a "Baby Daddy"

All the shit ya'll been through
And she still can't get through to you
Steady stressing that real talk in ya' ears
But the talk always ends with her in tears
See the shit that kills me is you think she's ya' enemy
But she's the one praying every day because she got your babies
She's never been perfect, never professed to be
But she was yo' rider, yo' friend, hell she was yo' family
She would have given you the shirt off her back, and froze in the cold
But the image, the girls, and friends made you fold
If she would have known things would be like this
She never would have sealed the deal with a nine month kiss
See one thing you failed to tell was how real she kept it
But you never neglected to tell the lies of your version, to that friend list of 2,000 skeptics
All the nights ya'll talked, all the times ya'll fought
But never once did she totally abandon your existence
She had to walk away!
And separate herself from the drama and mischief
See, she can't keep condoning the things that a Negro do wrong
And she can't raise her kids in a broken home
So yes, she gave you the walking papers in hopes you could get it right
Struggling to raise your kids, while you're nowhere in sight
You telling everyone that she's the reason for your absence
But neglecting to let them know how she never asked for a thing
But the consistency of your presence

She was strong enough to separate the two, and not cause any drama
Being a man's woman versus being his baby mama
Now, don't get it confused, my brothers, cause this is not a slander or diss
This is just the things that have affected her long term, hit and miss
Let me tell you again, she gets down on her knees and prays for you every day she breathes air
She's nothing without you, so, no matter the hell, she care
She wasn't made to hate
The world you brought her, she'll always appreciate
She could never hate you
The most beautiful parts of you and her has gotten her through
One, two, and then there was a third
She isn't holding a grudge over a thing she ever went through or heard
It's bigger than that and always will be
I speak for her in saying 'I could never hate my baby's daddy..."

Fatherless

Absent fathers don't upset me
It's the ones who bring inconsistency
I won't bash you because just as you chose me, I chose you
But now we both have a job to do
You were in the room, in love, the same way as me
Didn't you grow up without a daddy?
How selfish of you to have your child suffer the same fate
It's not all my responsibility to take!
I don't want any drama and I'm not here to divvy out none
But raising your children without your help isn't always fun
Whether you left or I did, is irrelevant
The fact that these children need both parents is very
prevalent
Who led you to believe that your presence wasn't
necessary?
Fatherless kids is becoming a little too damn ordinary...

It is what it is

You planted a seed
And left it to die
You out your mind
If you'll be the reason, I watch him cry
I won't beg, I won't ask, and it's not my job to instruct
Cause baby, In God we trust
I'm woman enough to handle it all, with or without your
assistance
But don't be astonished when the thought of you is
non-existent
See you want a chick that's going to beg you to be a man
Walking around here like you weren't once my biggest fan
You knew I would leave, I told you that
I know my worth, and it wasn't lining up with how you act
But all that is said and done
And we have a son
Frankly, damn if you don't, damn if you do
Holla at us when you're ready
And we'll pray it's not too late for you.

Why can't we co-parent?

All these years have passed
I've grown quite a bit, and maybe you have as well
I'll be the first to admit, this journey hasn't always been swell
It's been eye-opening, life changing and made me who I am
But I'm beginning to wonder, can I really raise a boy into a man
I mean it's been done many times, so this time will be no different
But I don't see why it's been so hard for us to co-parent
You've made mistakes and so have I
We've been best friends and arch enemies
But none of that changes the fact that we made beautiful babies
I've let you live carefree and did your part
I'd be lying if I didn't say, every blue moon it hurts my heart
I don't need your help but your kids definitely do
Open your eyes, this is bigger than me and you
I could care less about your new life
It wasn't a part of God's plan for me to be your partner, or wife
I'm far from bitter and I pray you are doing well
I deserve to be happy and free, just as you do too,
We've put each other through enough hell
But the fact of the matter is
What about your kids?
You've missed all the birthday parties, doctor's appointments, and basketball games
It's way past time for some things to change
I was never looking for you to be perfect
Dedicated and consistent, yes
But life is tricky, and the lessons are given after the tests
Each year they grow older and this world grows colder
There are things you hold that I can't teach

Put your pride down and your selfishness out of reach
Yea, I'm hell on wheels but I'm real
And you're no angel, but who cares how we feel
Truth of the matter is, we are family, and always will be
And our children deserve the best parts of you and me
Look at our daughter, she looks just like your twin
If we just worked together, then we could all win
I'm not asking for much, but for you to see what should come natural
Nothing I've said is far from factual
I think in some way I'd feel less of a mother if I didn't even bother
And I'd be lying still, if I ever said that at some point my children didn't need their father.

CHAPTER 3

Melanin matters

Dear Kings,

There is nothing on the face of this earth more beautiful to
me, than you
I see your potential, but what about you?
I'm speaking to your soul
So hear me when I say,
For you I bow down to my knees and every day, I pray
As the head of my household
The foundation of my race
So many of you, we have lost, because you failed to take
your place
Only so much blame can we continue to place on "the
others"
But look in the mirror, and what do you see my brother?
Do you see what I do?
Do you feel what I feel?
Understand! To the world, you ARE a big deal!
You are bigger than the cliché's and stereotypes
You are above the drugs, abuse, and political hype
Unleash your mind and take the rusty chains off your spirit
This is your heart talking to you, I want you to hear it.
I see the beauty in you, the strength, and your resilience
The charisma, the passion, your *above* average brilliance.
I am NOT your enemy, I would never harm you
It's my job to be your life, the main reason that you live
I'm here to be your peace, I came from your rib
Dark skin, with a perfect stature
Posture made specifically for a throne
I see the king in you,
I love you, I need you, and I can't do this alone
This is what you need to hear
Know it and live it because it's real

It's what my *sista's* are afraid to say because of the pain we feel
On any given day, I could tear you apart with my words,
and cut you down with my eyes
But lay in my bed in tears because for you, my heart still cries
From the plantation to the white house you've been a threat
Because nobody fears average, read the laws Willie Lynch set
I see the king in you, I bore you, and I am your mother, your
sister, and wife too
But if you don't see what I see, what is a Queen to do?

Little Brown Girl

One time for all the little brown girls
Shout out to all of you, all over the world
I see your determination, your desperation to be
above-average
It isn't a soul that can look so beautiful carrying such
baggage
Disrespected, neglected, and shamed by your own kind
But to still stand tall and embracing life to tell the world "I'm fine"
Negative perceptions of you world-wide, more now than
we've ever seen
But little brown girl, don't let that make you forget you are
still a queen
Despite what the others may say
It's little brown girls like you who helped pave the way
Little brown girls like Rosa, Oprah, Maya, and Michelle
That made it their business to represent us all very well
You see, you have inherited so many attributes and attitude
Rosa's back bone, Oprah's intelligence, and Maya's depth
and poetic magnitude
And let's not forget how Michelle was the epitome of a first
lady
A little brown girl with poise, elegance, and much swag baby
Little brown girl, always keep your head high and remain
true to who you are
Never let the world's stereotypes and statistics create a
wound or a scar.

Little Brother

Little brother don't go out in the street
It's men out there that want to see you get beat
Little brother watch those folks you call your friend
They'll only leave you six feet in the end
Little brother stay out of the view of the blue lights
Some of those people only want to try and pick a fight
That's a fight you may never win
It's not about you, little brother
It's about the color of your skin
Little brother, go to school and read all your books
Little brother, don't listen to the people shouting you're
destined to become a crook
Little brother, there are people out there who want to see
you in pain
You have everything to lose, and they have plenty to gain
Listen to me little brother, when I say they will try you
They will first say you are ADHD and tell mama you need
medicine too
Little brother, listen to me, because that's only the beginning
They'll put you on their basketball teams and have you think
you are winning
And that's ok little brother, because with talent you can go far
But be careful little brother if later on, they put the blue lights
on your car
I could tell you to do what they say, and don't give 'em no strife
But sadly little brother, I can't promise you, they'll spare your life
Little brother, this world is a cruel and unusual place
But little brother, you are made of tough skin, tenacity, and
strength to run this race
Little brother, you are necessary, one of a kind, and
specially made
Little brother, Little brother, WAKE UP, don't let your existence
fade.

It's History Time

I'm sick of social media protests, key board wars, and
coined phrases
Where are you social media lawyers, when people are
fighting cases?
See what's going on is bigger than your opinion or some
popular trend
There are lives at stake, from death, to war, and lawyers who
defend
It's not all about race, it's more to it than that
You can't always play that card
While using the same methods in a verbal attack
The things we are up against aren't all opposing oppositions
Stop acting like we aren't our own worst enemies
Against each other, selling souls for top-notch positions
Don't get it misconstrued, not saying we weren't placed in
the "bucket"
But A LOT of "us" act like we love our culture,
But get to a certain tax bracket and then say "fuck it"
I don't want to start at the top of the totem pole
Because that can sometimes be redundant
Let's pay homage to the youth,
The ones who hold the future's abundance
Ditch the mentality that's gotten us absolutely nowhere
Rosa, Martin, and Malcom got us all the rights we wanted
So you can no longer say what isn't considered fair
It's time to take responsibility for one another
And issues we've began to create amongst ourselves
It's time to educate, study, and intensely read beyond
what's been left upon the shelves
It's time to celebrate what we've earned
Instead of mourning what we lost

It's time we acknowledge
Pay our respects to those who truly paid the cost
It's time to put the guns down
Stop making everything a black on black debate
It's time to stop leaving the youth in the hands of an
incomplete fate
It's time to build up the communities from the inside out
It's time to become the model citizens that you hear about
It's time to stop looking for another Obama and wishing for
another first lady like Michelle
When you have that power, and the ability to be, before
history repeats itself.

A Black Woman's Pain

Master! Take me back one-hundred years
I need to take a walk down the trail of tears
It's some things I left behind
Listen up, I got some serious things on my mind
I left my family unit, the unity we once stood for
The ability to still smile, even though we may have been poor
I left behind the rods that didn't spare my children
I left behind the truth, how things really happen
I left my son's independence and my daughter's feminine side
I walked away with self-righteous, entitlement
A foolish sense of black pride
I left behind my husband, my protector, somewhere along
the way
Which has left me independent, but bitter, or so "they" say
He was taken from me, beaten, and left for dumb or dead
I left my sense of history and stored a bunch of lies in my head
I left my friends, you know, the ones who wouldn't leave
each other to die
Now I'm constantly watching the company I keep
Because the devil is a lie
I'm sick of this
Trying to raise my babies, to essentially become my enemy
By that I mean, my anger with the black man
I've been taught and conditioned to follow that Willie Lynch
guy's plan
I'm not afraid to say, that something is definitely wrong
Put these issues in an anthem, and call it a song
I'll sing it loud on the freedom train
Singing "I'm a black woman that's left my heritage behind
Because of it I'm IN PAIN"!!!

CHAPTER 4

Silent Fury

Behind the Curtains

There is a lot that goes on behind silence
People think because you don't react that there is no emotion
But the emotion is very real, living in a controlled environment waiting to kill
So intense, that the reaction would be almost fatal
Picture the woman sitting in the dark room holding her chest rocking like a cradle
That kind of pain is called heartache
You feel everything break by break
It's the things that go unsaid that tend to have the most weight
It's the hearts that don't speak that have suffered the most breaks
People want you to be like them, fit into their mold, and create a scene
That's what is socially accepted of love and pain, and the things that it can bring
People think fighting for what you love is a display of affection
All that energy used in the wrong direction
Silence they hate, because of fear of the unknown
They borrow anger from the devil at a high interest loan
Ya'll could never understand the meaning behind all of this
If I truly told you what goes on, the point you would still miss.

Full Moon

They say if you can't sleep at night
And you wonder why, God may be trying to tell you
something
So on a night like tonight
I pick up my pen and pad, and go for what I know
Emotions like the tide, spilling on the shore as an overflow
Looking for the nearest exit or place to go
What do I say, hell what do I feel
Mind in shambles, heart on repeat, and words at a standstill
A beat in my spirit, my pen on move
Desperately crying out for expression
And can't catch the groove
All that to say what?
Do they understand the struggle of girl-hood?
And the change into a woman
Or maybe that's unnecessary, just a pointless line
Maybe just something I made up
Something that sounds good, and hell it rhymes
With ears that bleed, and a mouth that can commit a one
eighty seven
Makes for an interesting collaboration like the rulers of hell
and heaven
God as my witness, I can't make any of this up
This life is like a poker game, and I'm running out of luck
But you wouldn't be able to tell, nope you just can't tell
My conscience is clear, but my heart will rot in hell
I'm laughing, like where does she get this kind of crazy
verbiage and thought process
The kids in the neighborhood think she's crazy, but the
womb bearer says she's genius

Who gets their ass up at three a.m. with a full moon in the window writing silly little rhymes?
Well I guess I do, because God woke me up, and said "It's time"....

4 A.M

Silence, black skies, and in the houses souls lay sleep
White walls, the dull roar of the heater, and the clock hand
on creep
The hour when time, like death at a funeral, stands still
The hour when criminals crawl about
In search of blood from their next kill
What is considered day but still called night
Somewhere in between the eerie darkness hides the light
It's too early to call it night
And too early to call it morning
Too soon to say it's safe
And too late to send out any warning
That time is now, as I write this down
A spirit awakes me suddenly out of my sleep
And like the clock hand, down the hall, I creep
The spirit says, like death at a funeral, this hour will stand still
So as if you know it's your time, begin to write your will
Like a criminal crawling about in search of blood
As my emotions begin to bleed ink
And I won't stop until I've had the last drink
The spirit has made twilight a ubiquity for me
Too late to not be sleeping and too early to be awake
weeping
At this hour the spirit possesses full control
Some have called it the "hour of the souls"
For me it's simply the precious hour that the lord allowed my
mother to bring me here
The same hour he strangely awakens me and tells me to
write the things I hear....

Silent Fury

I said this time I wouldn't hold back
I'm taking breaths, leaving them fatally wounded, like a
heart attack
I got some things to say and I'm not leaving until they feel me
Hear me, breathe me, and I know you will relate to me
Been quiet for quite some time
And silence has become my number one "frenemy"
God said it's power in the tongue to be careful what you say
So I learned to hold in the real deal stuff, and simply pray
These devils attack me all night and they stalk me all day
The devil in me could have been aired dirty laundry
Used my darkness to fuel my light
But mama said "don't do it child, you are way too bright"
She said "you never know what you learn by being quiet
and getting still"
And she has never told me wrong because she know how I feel
They came for me every time they had an opportunity
And every time I let them breathe
And this is what created my silent fury
Sometimes it's the things that are left unsaid that you have
to be able to hear
Read between the blurred lines and they will appear
Seeing is believing, but looks can be deceiving
And behind ever silent grave, is a family that's grieving

You missed it.....

Logged In

Are you really who you say you are?
Or just a figment of a post?
This new wave of technology has become quite gross
Subliminal sentences, hidden objectives, and cruel public
outbursts
Messy drama, infidelity, cruel intentions, and identity thirst
Shout out to those constantly shedding light
And speaking from a place of educated existence
That doesn't include those that throw stones but live in glass
houses
Excuse me while I jump fences
Or those that log in just to protest,
You know? The black lives matter, and maybe homosexual
lives too
The friends we never see at a community rally or panel
discussion
Until it happens to you
What are you doing besides utilizing an email and a
password?
Stop telling me what you saw on a video,
Or on the TV, what you heard.
Put your boots on the ground, and start with the youth of today
Begin with the ones who are struggling with disabilities and
disadvantages each day
Stop logging in and posting that one time you helped the
needy
When it's the least you could do, seeing as how you've
always been greedy
For attention, that is, to be validated and emancipated
From the brutality of your own insecurities
Stop logging in just to keyboard kill your own communities.

Symptoms of a demoniac

Tough but tired
These feelings are about to be fired
This headache is about to exit
It's time to fully address it
The symptoms of pain
Nothing more to lose, but plenty to gain
You, you and ya'll ain't got a clue what it's like
Every single day is a battle zone, an all-out fight
Things hurt, things aren't the same
These people love you but every day they change
I can't see the forest for the trees
Life is poison, it's killing me
And not a soul understands
Rip me inside out, I need the ego of a man
The hell of trying to adapt to mistakes, decisions, and the universe
The blessing keep coming disguised as a curse
All these facades and distorted views
Lord I'm on my knees hanging on for dear life, screaming from the pews
Save me from my own overthought mind
Help me lord please, I'm running out of time....

CHAPTER 5

Poetic Prayers

Lord, Thank you

Lord, I thank you for another day
I just want to say hallelujah, because you keep making a way
Bless your holy name for courage and strength
For the armor you cover me in, for the things I'm up against
Keeping my mind, and my heart balanced and stable
My dependence solely on you, because lord I know that you're able
Sometimes, like how I get quiet so you can hear my heart screams
The devil attacks me even in the midst of my dreams
I have realized there are some things not a soul in this would could ever understand
But oh dear lord, I know that you always have a plan
With tears in my eyes, and a bible at my side
I know to your presence I can run and hide
So many things ravish my mind and my heart is still plagued with occasional pain
But your word dear God it has kept me sane
Thank you my God, with a humble heart and spirit I say thank you over and over again
I'm truly blessed to have you as my very best friend.

So I Pray

Every day I pray
Because it takes the pain away
It eases the mind
And you begin to learn that things really do get better with time
See life will hand you lemons, and with them you can make lemonade
But even if it's cold as ice, it's no match for a hot day under the sun with no shade
So, I pray…
Pray the lord give me peace
And allow me to rise each morning from underneath the sheets
Pray the lord make me strong
To keep my mind intact from all the things that will or could go wrong
Every single day, I pray…
I've seen a lot and I've heard many things
Pain, sadness, and misunderstandings is what life can sometimes bring
I remember the days when I thought, from the breaks, my heart would never heal
Devil had my mind, and spirit on what seemed like over-kill
Can you believe I wanted to die? Just to escape it all
The turmoil was so intense
Heart and mind in shambles
And none of it seemed to make any sense
So, I pray….
Pray that the lord keeps me patient
Steadfast, and full of persistence each day
I've seen him change so many things
And happiness and peace is what it all seems to bring

Pray the lord allows me to forgive because my hurt is not my story
I'm the evidence of things not seen, but hoped for,
And for that I give God the glory
Every day, I pray...
Because I know the lord hears me, I know that prayer changes things,
And deliverance, to what seems like a time in hell
Is what prayer can bring...

Just when you thought

Just when you thought that you were through
Just when you thought "What am I going to do?"
Just when you thought "I can't take it anymore!"
God said "yes, you can" and opened another door.
Just when you thought, "I've had all I can take"
Just when you thought "I have nothing left to give!"
God said "Yes", and gave you one-hundred more reasons
to live
Just when you thought "I've been hurt beyond what can be
repaired"
When you thought love was just a word and mutual feelings
were rare
Just when you thought, this is just the way it's supposed to be
God said "No, it isn't", and showed you the people that love you
Just as much as he
Just when you thought "I can't pay all these bills"
Just when you thought the doctor would have to prescribe
stronger pills
Just when you thought, that your problems were your own
God said "No" and showed you that you weren't all alone
Just when you thought that your faith had ran out
And the devil stepped in
Just when you thought "I'll put my misery to an end"
Just when you thought, it was all over for you
God said "NO, get on your knees and pray and that's all
you ever have to do."

Supplication

Walked the floor all night
With Satan sitting in plain sight
Your heart is heavy, mind twisted, plagued with all your fears
Eyes swollen, and full of dried up tears
A hundred different supplications
And a book full of intimate verses
Searching and begging for any revelation
The eerie dark shadows you see are evil himself
But you trust in the lord like nobody else
Before you let those fears try to devour you
Before you let another tear fall
Drop to your knees and pray over it all
Ask for his help and lay down your burdens
For he is a burden bearer
A heavy load carrier
A bridge over troubled waters
And if you feel he doesn't hear you
Then you just pray harder
You pray until you can't any more
Until the blood from your knees
Grips the grooves in the floor
Until the devil is rebuked from the sound of his name, you
are crying
All I'm asking is for you to just try him.

I Know God!!!

I know it is Christ that strengthens me
And I cancel all plans of my arch enemy
He'll take the enemies against me
And make them my footstool
He'll make a ministry out of the things that were meant to be cruel
I'll fight in prayer, and worship God, no matter the situation
I am who GOD says I am
His beautiful, unique, creation
A lot of things got to me, and some things tried to break my spirit
But God is the head of my life,
What his word says, is the gospel
Anything less, I don't want to hear it
I'm not, nor will I ever be, what the world sees as perfect
But I know the Lord loves me anyway, because I AM worth it
Anytime I want to doubt my own purpose and strength
I think of the mountains he moved, that my back was up against
I know where my help comes from, and I'll never hide that
I know who comes to my rescue when the devil tries to attack
I know who I can call on, in the midnight hour or the middle of the day
I know that the only distance between us, is just one prayer away
I know that without him, I'm nothing, and nothing I do is complete
I KNOW that God will propel me
With him there is no acceptance or expectation of defeat.

EPILOGUE

Beautiful butterfly why don't you fly,
She whispers "It's this life that has almost got me beat
I'm on a mission to succeed, but the wind and storms have
me feeling like I can barely breathe
You see "they" all admire my beauty, rareness, and my
strength to fly
I have to admit that sometimes it's a pleasure, and then
there are days when I just want to land and cry
Everyone sees the outside, but doesn't realize what it took to
get this way
What I came from didn't happen overnight, just as Rome
wasn't built in a day
The world see's the beauty after what evolution brings
Without the idea of knowing that I went through such
change
And still I can't wait to see my wings….

Printed in the United States
By Bookmasters